POEMS AND PRAISE

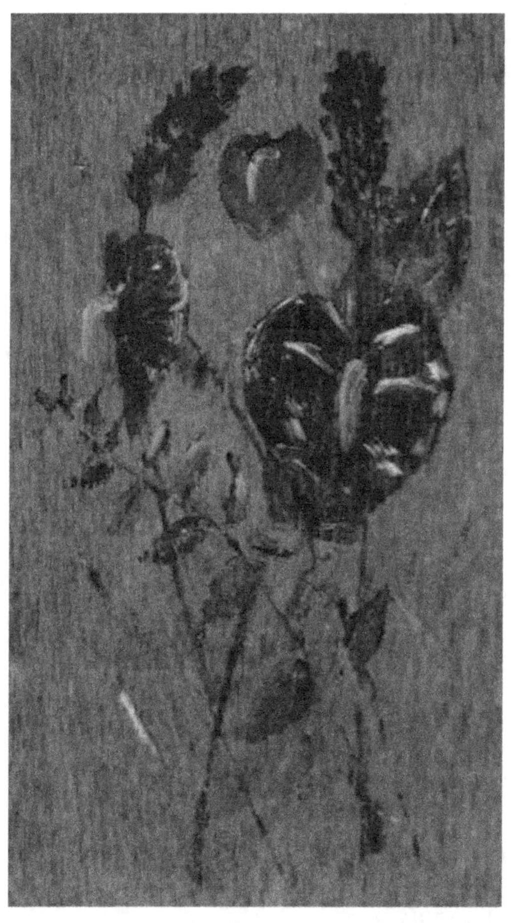

By
Gertrude R. Anderson

Poems and Praise
By
Gertrude R. Anderson

M.O.R.E. Publishers Corp.
P.O. Box 38285
Spanish Lake, MO 63138
www.MOREPublishers.biz
MOREPublishersCO@AOL.com

Copyright © 1976, 2010, Gertrude R. Anderson.

All rights reserved. No part of this book may be reproduced or used in any form, by any means electronically or mechanically, including photocopying, recording, or storing information in retrieval systems without written permission of the author.

Printed in the United States.
ISBN 978-0-9758549-1-4
ISBN 0-9758549-1-7
Library of Congress Control Number: 2010903900

Inside art by Terry Holt, Memphis, Tennessee
Cover designs by M.O.R.E. Publishers

Contributors:
Dorothy C. Anderson
Mildred R. Crutcher
Anjanette Hall
Patricia A. Jamison
Naomi Baker Richmond
Vera Taylor Richmond

CONTENTS

Black History

Introduction

Words are powerful. The purpose for writing POEMS AND PRAISES was to inspire people to live a life of peace, love, and Godliness.

No one has been more influential in using words to inspire than Jesus Christ and the psalmist David in the Bible. Their words of Love, Righteousness, and Forgiveness are the cornerstone of our Faith.

Powerful words have also been used to shape our laws, to establish rights, and to advance civilization as we know it.

We hope that the writers in this book will continue to encourage the readers to use talents to help spread the good news of Jesus Christ, and to give God the glory.

Let God guide you.
I know that you will do well,
and you will be blessed by reading
POEMS AND PRAISE.

In Obedience and Love,
Gertrude R. Anderson

Foreword

Thanks to our Christian writers who used their talents of poetic and spiritual expressions to create this body of work entitled ***Poems and Praise.***

A Moment of Dedication

POEMS AND PRAISE is dedicated

- To my family, who did not complain when I sometimes shut them out while I read a book, and did not take time to visit.

- To my son Gary and his wife Debra who took time to read and encourage me in my writing and made comments where needed; to make the book readable, and to make sure I met other writers who gave me encouragement to continue doing what I enjoy.

- To those who told me, "I really enjoyed what you wrote."

- To our youth, in their search for truth, peace, and contentment in a modern day society.

Love and Comfort

"LOVE"

Love is forgiving.
Love is understanding.
Love is patience.
Love is free.

When God directs your life, it is easy.
In the good times, in the bad times, and in Ancient times,
Love is constant.

Love holds all things together, and makes them right,
in God's sight.

It (love) strengthens our will, guides our way, gives us
peace, fulfills our joy, and brings us closer to God - our
ultimate destination; for He is LOVE!

"This is my commandment, that
Ye love one another as I have loved you."
John 15:2

Gertrude R. Anderson
poet

"A Blessed Lady"

A lady, who loves the Lord, is a joyful treasure.
She is priceless. Her value is beyond measure.
Her quiet and meek spirit, and her loving heart,
Not only delight men, but they are precious to God.

Following the Shepherd, she walks in the light.
Her steps are ordered by day and by night.
Totally trusting the grace, and the wisdom of God,
She rests in the comfort of his staff and rod.

As she walks after truth, excellence, and beauty,
Her work becomes a joy, not toil and duty.
She receives praise by the works of her hands,
And gladly shares what she understands.

She is a woman of prayer, purpose, and power.
She knows the value of worship and praise.
While basking in His presence, hour after hour,
She commits to her purpose, to her plans, and to her ways.
She casts all her of cares at the Savior's feet.
That is where her joy is complete.
She finds grace for whatever the day is demanding,
And abides in peace, that passeth all understanding,
By His grace.

"Every wise woman buildeth her house,
but the foolish plucketh it down, with her own hands."
Proverbs 14:1

Naomi B. Richmond
poet

"Things That Brighten the Spirit"

Beauty around you, flowers, pictures, etc.
Prayer and Praise and Meditation
No feelings of guilt or wrong-doing
Doing good and helping others
Being around positive people
Seeing a job well done
An answered prayer
Well-being of family and friends;
No bad news
No wars, nor catastrophes;
Peace

All of these things may not occur at the same time, but our peace with God is the most important one of all.

Gertrude R. Anderson
poet

"Victorious"

Be strong in the Lord, and the power of his might.
Keeping the faith is your only fight.
Put on the whole armor of God
To protect your mind, and guard your heart.

Keeping God's truth, righteousness, and peace,
Causes Satan's torment to cease.
The word of God, praise, worship, and fervent prayer,
Will give you devil-stomping power to spare.

When Satan comes around
Talking his baloney,
Overcome him with the blood of the Lamb,
And with the word of your testimony.

Christ claimed the victory at Calvary long ago;
The devil is a liar, a loser and a defeated foe.

"For whosoever is born of God overcometh the world, and this is the victory that overcometh the world, even our faith."
1 John 5:4

Grace be unto you,
Naomi B. Richmond
poet

"Standing Before God"

If the Lord called you home today, could you stand before His throne and say, "Lord, I tried to obey your commandments and help someone find you along the way"?

Could you say, "I treated every man as my brother and every woman as my sister, who walked with me on the road to Salvation", and mean it?

Could you say, "I wiped the tears from the eyes of a desperate child or assisted an elderly person who stumbled along life's path way", with half-blind eyes?

Could you say, "I helped a young mother who struggled to survive, or showed concern for a family that society seemed to have forgotten"?

Could you say, "I spoke the truth and did not ignore the innocent because I did not want to get involved, and I was not a stumbling block to anyone who sought God's will and way"?

Could you say, "I praised God for His goodness and honored His name in my conversation and was led by His Spirit in all of my decisions"?

Could you say that "I did not steal the praise from another or declared their work to be my own to all who would listen, because of jealousy"?

Could you hold your head up and face God in His Holy presence and say, "Yes Lord, I did all I could to do your will even though sometimes it was difficult and my so-called friends walked away"?

I remembered. I remembered that You said in Your word, "If you love me, keep my commandments."

I remembered that you would write my name on a stone that no one could read it but me. You said, "I'll be with you always, even to the end of the world", and I believed you!

"As for me, I will behold thy face in righteousness:
I shall be satisfied when I awake with thy likeness."
Psalms 15:17

In Obedience and Love,
Gertrude R. Anderson
petitioner

“Stop and Say Thanks”

Must we always complain about the things we do not have?
Must we always be more concerned with ourselves and never for others?
Must we always question Him about our life and constantly ask Him why?
Must we always have what we want?

Stop and thank Him!
Thank God for all the little things we do have.
Thank Him for letting us live to see this day.
Thank Him for all the good things we do have.
Thank Him for being our protector and comforter.

Whatever we do, please stop and thank God!

“Giving thanks always for all things unto God, the Father in the name of our Lord Jesus Christ.”
Ephesians 5:20

Anjanette Hall
poet

“Getting the New Year in Focus”

Focus!
Focus on Christ not on circumstances.
Fretting and complaining, blaming, worrying, and running won’t help at all.
Love, Joy, and Peace are found in Jesus.

Focus!
Focus on the sovereignty of God, not on the will of man.
Try to see, and follow God’s plan for your life.

Focus!
Focus on the positive results, not on the personal pain.

Personal inconvenience often speeds up God’s purpose.
Rejoice that God is ever-present in your life,
and that He has it all under His control.

Live above your circumstances.
Look up to Jesus.
Live victoriously and glorify God!

By His Grace,
Naomi B. Richmond
poet

"Eyes - Windows of the Soul"

The Lord made me to see His beauty all around;
The grass of the fields and the leaves on the ground.

See the shadow of the trees
When the leaves are blowing in the summer breeze.

Oh! What a joy that fills my soul,
When I look up and see the clouds and wonder,
"Where are they going or where do they go? Or
Are they up in Heaven where they have been before?"

The wind will blow them away
But they will return again and again, someday.

The Lord controls them, just as He made the whole world
and its beauty for the eyes to see.
Jesus has all the power because He even made me!

"To everything there is a season
and a time to every purpose under the heaven."
Ecclesiastics 1:1

Mildred R. Crutcher
poet

"Easter"

Do you know that Jesus died?
But do you know He's still alive?
Touch your heart and feel His grace;
Can't you feel Him in this place?

He's bringing Peace and Joy sublime,
And filling up this heart of mine.
Jesus died that we might live.
He lived and showed us His perfect will.

He came to see us when we were lost
And showed us the way without any cost.
He rolled away the door to the tomb,
And let us know that He'll come back soon!

And he said unto Jesus, "Lord remember me when thou comest into thy kingdom. And Jesus said unto him, "Verily I say unto thee, today shalt thou be with me in Paradise."
Luke 23:43

In Obedience and Love,
Gertrude R. Anderson
psalmist

"Comfort"

Soon I'll be making a journey.
I'm going all by myself.
Jesus will be waiting; I won't need anybody else.

There will be peace all around me.
No more trouble will there be.
Heaven's doors will be opened wide
and I will joyfully walk inside.

There will be happiness and love,
and all the Angels up above.
Mothers will be smiling and talking
while friends and loved ones are out, about walking.

I'll be so happy when I take to the air;
I'm looking forward to seeing you there.
When I take my journey and my soul is set free
I'll shout Halleluiah when the Lord of Lords says,
"Welcome home servant, and come sit by me."

"For His anger endureth but a moment;
in his favour is life;
weeping may endure for a night,
but joy cometh in the morning."
Psalms 30:5

In Obedience and Love,
Gertrude R. Anderson
poet

"Comfort, In a Time of Sorrow"

When I leave you,
remember dear loved ones,
I came from a SPIRIT world and now I have returned.
This is my earthly house you see lying here.
God gave it to me so I could live
and share my life with you for awhile
and now my Spirit
has returned to God who created it.

But don't be sad,
I have not left you.
I'm still here in Spirit.
When you remember my face,
you are still seeing me.
When you remember my voice,
you are still hearing me.
When you remember my joy, and my pain,
you are remembering all that my life has brought to you
in the past.
I pray that my Spirit will guide you in its understanding.

And when time has claimed your body and age has
clouded your thoughts,
my Spirit will remain.
It will appear in the faces and actions of the way I talked,
and the way I walked in those who share the same bodily
inheritance — my family.
Even though it may seem impossible sometimes, even in
your condition you will see my face and remember the
person that I was,
if only for a second.

When your time has been spent here on Earth,
we will gather again at our creator's feet
and see God's son, Jesus.
We will rejoice and say, "Thank You, Lord. Our love for one another has only made our meeting again, a time of unspeakable joy!"

****

A Prayer

Heavenly Father,
we come before You today,
asking for Your blessings and mercy.

Please fill us with your Spirit and with your love.
Fill our hearts with compassion and forgiveness.
Let us all be one
in your Holy Son,
in brotherly love, and in unity.

Cast aside all doubts, hatred and strife;
As we bow in your presence, in Your Holy sight.

Fill us with your Spirit;
Fill us with your love.
Please fill our hearts with compassion,
Forgiveness and love.

"Pray without ceasing."
1 Thessalonians 5:17

In Obedience and Love,
Gertrude R. Anderson
petitioner

“Precious Memories”

When I was a little girl, I enjoyed visiting a childless neighbor who had a fenced area of her yard that she called ‘The Park’.

Inside, there was a great tree with a swing that hung from a giant limb, and there was a picnic table. The ground was a carpet of lush green clover, a sheer delight to my bare feet.

I spent many happy hours there as we shelled beans or peas. I watched and played while she crafted her needlework.

She listened to my childish hopes and dreams and helped me to feel significant. I have many precious memories of Miss Loyce and the ‘Park’.

This memory centers around what I recall as being one of the most difficult times of my life and one of the most delicious meals I have eaten.

Several years ago I came from the hospital and was under such heavy sedation. I could hardly stand, much less prepare a meal for my family. Sister Cora Jones came over and fried chicken, cooked turnip greens and mashed potatoes, and made cornbread. It was absolutely outstanding!

I am sure that to her, this was just a simple form of kindness. However, it still stands out in my memory because she did for me what I couldn’t do at that particular time. Thanks Demp!

“The eyes of the Lord are in every place beholding the evil and the good.”
Proverbs 15:3

His love and mine,
Naomi Baker Richmond

"Things My Parents Taught Me"

My parents taught me how to cuddle and how to walk,
How to feed myself with a spoon and how to talk;
How to tie my shoes and put them on,
And to know the difference, when they are put on wrong;

How to make my bed and how to tell the time,
And hang my clothes straight, on a clothes line;
How to share with others and how to live;
When to be loud outdoors, and in church - be still!

How to care for my clothes and comb my hair;
How to be polite to others and not to stare;
How to be a friend and do well in school,
And not let any success turn me into a fool!

How to read the Bible and recognize God's grace,
How to respect my elders and give others space;
To walk with others and respect their wishes,
To love my neighbors and not dig ditches;

How to do my best in the work that I do,
To love myself so I'll learn to love you.
"Do not talk to strangers" or stay out late,
Not be a stumbling stone and not to hate;

To thank God for Jesus each day of my life,
For blessing my family and keeping down strife;
How to give to others and not always receive.
Yet there's one thing that they couldn't teach me -
When the Lord calls one of us home,
No one can teach how not to grieve!

In Obedience and Love,
Gertrude R. Anderson

Motherhood

"Mother"

A Mother is a Mother in so many ways!
It takes a Mother's love to make a house a home,
A place to be remembered
No matter where you roam.

It takes a Mother's patience,
To bring a child up in the world,
Her courage, and her cheerfulness,
To make a dark day bright.

It takes a Mother's thoughtfulness to mend the heart, and
her skill of endurance to mend little shirts and socks.

It takes a Mother's kindness to forgive,
When we error;

To sympathize when in trouble
And to bow her head in prayer.

It takes a Mother's wisdom to recognize our needs,
And reassurance by her loving words and deeds.

It takes a Mother's endless faith, confidence, and trust,
To guide us through the pitfall of selfishness and lust.

It takes a Mother to always be there when needed,
no matter what the problem is.
It takes the love of a Mother
that will never close the door
tight behind her children no matter what.

That is why in all this world,
There could not be another
Who could fulfill God's purpose completely,
As a God-fearing Mother.

A Mother is someone who touches your hand
And reaches your heart.

Vera Taylor Richmond
poet

"A Mother's Love"

A mother's love is the heart of a home.
She works when she doesn't feel like it.
She looks out for the total welfare of her children
and home.
She smiles when they smile,
hurts when they hurt.
She always prays for their well being.

Mothers never forget that God gave them a wonderful gift
when He gave them a child to love.
Many times the way may get rough
and the food get low,
but bread and water given from a loving Mother's hand is
like a feast of the finest food.

With her love,
her children will thrive and grow strong.
A Mother's love never dies.
It stays with her until her last breathe is gone.
Even then, the children's names will be on her lips,
begging God to have mercy on them,
and to keep them in His care.

God smiled on Mothers and created them in a special
way.
A child is situated next to its Mother's heart
from the beginning of its life
and lays on her heart
until the end of her life on earth by faith….beyond.

A loving mother will work to build up her children's self-esteem and faith in God.
She will not crush the self-esteem down and ridicule it in their eyes.

When discipline is given,
it is for their protection and knowledge
to prepare them for the test in life's journey.

Others may turn their back on a child - but a Mother will say, "No matter what the crime, that child is mine, and I love my child.

"For whosoever shall do the will of my Father which is in Heaven the same is my brother and sister and mother."
Matthew 12:50

In Obedience and Love,
Gertrude R. Anderson

"A Mother Says 'Thanks'"

A young Mother stood with tears in her eyes.
Her two sons now stood near, by her side.
She said, "Many prayers have been said to have them
    stand here.
Many thanks I am giving to friends far and near."

Thanks,
To the preacher who taught them that God answers
    prayer;
To the teacher that showed them the world's beauty out
    there;
To their friends who stood always by their side
And told them the truth when all others lied;
To the old man down the road who gave them advice,
And helped them to recognize what's wrong and what's
    right.

There are things that young men must learn as they grow -
The value of manhood and what they should know.

Thanks,
To the coach at the school who taught them fair play;
To the students who helped them bear their burdens each
    day;
To the girls who cheered them when down in the blues;
To the neighbors who wrote them and shared home-town
    news.
To the cousins who said we wish you were here,
And kept their hopes up with prayers and good cheer.
We thank everyone who helped them stay strong,
And helped me to bear it until they came home.

"God bless you, my dear friends", this young Mother said.
"My dear sons are home and not with the dead.
War is hurtful and soldiers know well,
To kill another person is a slow living hell".

God help us to settle our problems and faults,
With peace and forgiveness and love as we ought.
I know God has heard me, He's never left me yet.
With God's Grace and mercy, life is good as it gets.

My thanks will forever be in prayer and in song.
I know it's God's blessing that my dear sons came home.

Dedicated to Sister Nonnie Ingram Ship
and her two soldier Sons.
God blessed their return!

In Obedience and Love,
Gertrude R. Anderson

“A Mother’s Encouragement”

None of us are perfect though we try to do our best,
But some of our children really put us to the test.

Keep your hand in God’s hand
And He will see you through.
God will always lead,
And guide you in everything you do.

Just make sure you keep Him foremost
Every single day,
And please, always remember
How important it is to pray.

A child is truly a blessing
That God has sent your way.
So as you teach them, and shape them,
Please remember just to pray.

As storms come into your life,
And please believe me they surely will,
For Satan is busy,
And our children he’s out to steal –
Just pause and take a deep breath,
And if they start to stray,
Place them back in the Master’s hand, and
Pray, and Pray, and Pray!

Dorothy C. Anderson
poet

"A Mother's Story"
(Prose)

Today, I looked at a young picture of my Mother. Her beautiful hair now has turned gray. I asked her "Why is this so?"

These are some of the words she had to say. "Many people say that gray hair comes from worry, but I say some of this gray comes from time and circumstances that no one can control. If you live long enough, you will get gray. That is in God's plan.

"As for my gray, it may have come from watching changes that we can't understand, like watching loved ones go off to war and praying that they will come home again.

"A few strands of gray may have come from the constant job of keeping one's house in order and helping others who had more troubles than I had. Other strands of gray came from bringing children into an uncertain world of change, growth and diversity, with ideas and customs, and trying to adjust to the differences.

"Speeding up the process of going gray, we Mothers are watching our young people groping their way through the lessons of life and growing in unfamiliar waters.

"Many of these strands came from tragedies we endured in our day and the news media accounts that troubled our peace.

"We now stand and watch a world change before our very eyes. Things that were once considered wrong are now considered right in many lives.

"Each strand of hair in a mother's head tells a story of its experience and how it came to be there. If they could talk, they would tell you that time has its own rewards and lessons to learn; that nothing but God's love and His Majesty last forever.

"We older Mothers know that our peace is in God's hands. We learned this early in life and prayed for guidance in every walk of life.

"Some day you will have to give an account of your life. One of God's Ten Commandments tells us, 'Thou shall have no other God before Me'."

Now when I look at the gray in any Mother's hair I see it as a testimony of God's gift of love, patience, and wisdom that He gives to Mothers. I feel blessed to be a part of that group.

"Quicken me after thy loving kindness so shall I keep the testimony of thy mouth."
Psalms 119:88

In Obedience and Love,
Gertrude R. Anderson

Adoration and Praise

"Songs of the Universe"

I hear the songs of the universe,
and the melodies are awesome!
The earth, wind, fire and water songs are beautiful beyond comparison.
The earth's music gives birth to plants, animals, trees, and food to its inhabitants.
The routine of spinning in space holds everything
together, and in place, thriving with a rainbow,
a promise from on High.

In the wind, I hear its song, and feel its presence.
It is heard when we breathe,
and then see it when it is a tornado skipping over the sky,
and dancing the dance of death and destruction over the land.
I hear the sound of birds as they ride the currents, singing as they go, hastening to their nesting places, with their own sense of direction.
I enjoy its breeze while sitting under a tree, enjoying the shade in the heat of the day.

Listen and you will hear the water sing.
See the waves as they crash against the solid rocks, and
the rain in a summer shower, gently falling from above.

I feel the snow flakes in their silence.
No two flakes alike.
Then I watch them come to rest, and turn to water on my flesh.
I listen to balls of sleet pelt my window panes as they float on a cold wave.
There is a water world hidden in the deep sea,

filled with fish, whales, seals, and many species, still
unknown, but they all call it “home”.
Up in the heavens, the moon guides the tides,
as they move in and out on distant shores.

Tears from my eyes,
the water where I hid in my mother’s womb;
the lemonade I drank from my cup,
add to the wonders of waters’ capabilities,
and its worth.

Last, but not least, behold the fire,
mighty and strong.
Its cleansing power and destructive power are twins in its actions.
It helps to create life, and help the earth maintain its responsibilities to its inhabitants.
Its rays of warmth gives birth to plants, trees, and food for man and beast alike.

High above in the universe resides a big ball of fire we call the Sun.
It is a fire that never goes out.
It creates and recreates itself over and over again since the beginning of time as we know it.

Yes, I hear the songs of the universe,
but one thing is certain; God is the creator of it all.
The melodies and songs they sing are no comparison to the songs the Angels sing in God’s presence – “Holy, Holy, Holy, Holy, Holy!”

"Praise"

Black people have always loved Music.
Every chance we get, we make music, and can make it with almost anything.
When there is nothing to make it with we use our hands and feet to keep the movement smooth, even in our work.
We also like motion as we make music.
Here is a hand clapping song with some motion.

Let's begin: It's called: "The Train To Glory."
I been traveling on this Christian Journey
I been walking it step by step
Carrying life's burdens on my shoulder
I just couldn't make it by myself
So I called on Jesus – the Son of God
To walk right by my side
Cause when the Heavenly train stops by here
Lord, I want to ride.

I been traveling this road a long time
Sometimes my soul get tired
I may not have done everything I should
But my God knows I tried
When my enemies knock me to my knees
God's grace did pick me up
I'm a witness He reached out and touched me
And He filled my bitter cup
Because I called on Jesus - the Son of God
To walk right by my side
Cause when the Heavenly train stops by here
Lord, I want to ride.

This train is Heaven's train
It runs on a track called Faith

The engine is powered by Jesus Himself
His schedule is never late
But you must be born again
Have your ticket in your hand
If we don't make it to the Promised Land
We've only ourselves to blame.
You just call on Jesus – the Son of God
To walk right by your side
Cause when the Heavenly Train stops by here
I Know, I Know, I Know
You want to ride.

Gertrude R. Anderson

"Thanksgiving"

Lord Jesus, daily I give thanks for all You've done.
In my life, You will always be number one.

First in my heart, first in my Spirit, first in my soul;
I have fully surrendered to the Holy Spirit's control.

Because You desire the very best for me;
I confidently offer all the rest of me.

Your counsel is always sure, wise and true.
How could anyone help but love You?

Thank You for guiding all of my days;
For saving me from my destructive ways.

For continuously uplifting me, until I could see;
The grace and beauty You bestowed upon me.

You made me a masterpiece, a piece of the Master;
The very thought makes my heart beat faster.

I'm Your original design, I'm one of a kind;
Created uniquely with Your purpose in mind.
Completely human, yet wonderfully divine.

I treasure all that I am in You;
I'm awed by all that You are in me.
This unique relationship has become my reality.

My anchor on life's stormy sea,
my fortress, my rock, my security.
For all I am, or ever hope to be,
I give thanks, honor, and praise to thee.

In Adoration
"Naomi"

Black History

1900's Cotton Field Cultivator

prose - Definition: Poetic Paragraphs

AFRICA!

- Home of the Black people
- Fed by the Nile, the longest river in the world
- The cradle of creation
- The founders of civilization
- Full of riches
- Unknown but to God
- The abundant sources of healing for every nation
- The Black and Brown Continent.
- First Man's home

Africa!

From generation to generation, species of every kind are growing and are nurtured by the rivers and the soil and the sun.
The life's blood of the past, commands it to live on!

Africa!

Hovering in a distant - like a precious jewel
Watched by the world for unknown answers to complex problems

Africa!

What is Africa to me you say?
To a child on American soil, I say in a heart beat, it is an inheritance, a blood tie, a culture hidden in my mind that appears sometimes out of nowhere. It is a surprise even to me. It is an emotion driven by a drum beat of a distant past; created by God who is the maker of all things.
He put His creations where He willed and where He has prepared.

Africa!

The home of my ancestors

A hidden Paradise in my mind
Our Beginning
Our Past
Our Anchor in time!
Africa!

"When thou art in tribulation
and all things are come upon thee,
even in the latter days,
if thou turn to the Lord thy God,
and shall be obedient unto His voice;
(For the Lord thy God is a merciful God;)
He will not forsake thee,
neither destroy thee,
nor forget the Covenant of thy fathers –
which He swore unto them."
Deuteronomy 4:30-31

In Obedience and Love,
Gertrude R. Anderson

“Suit of Armor”

Have you ever lived in a world with no harmony?
Have you ever lived in a world with no equal Liberty?
Have you ever lived in a world that you had to be better to
be good?
Have you ever lived in a world, misunderstood?
Have you ever lived in a world as a minority ruled by the
majority?

I am a person, who has felt discrimination not because of
my personality,
Gender or my generation,
But because of the suit of armor
That my Father chose to put on me.

Frowned upon because people felt I didn’t belong;
Looked down on because people felt I didn’t measure up;
Spit upon because I wouldn’t ‘kiss up’

I have had to sit in the back of a bus
And enter into a building through the ‘back only’ door
because I was labeled “Dirty and Black”.

I have had to wait to be last
All because of myths from the past.
Although many of my ancestors have passed on,
Some of their legacies still linger.

Some people have come to the realization
That “I am a part of the human nation,
One of God’s great creations”.
I am made in His image, I am proud to say.
Yes my skin is of bronze, my hair of wool,
And my soul is filled with only those things that are good.

You ask, “How have I survived the war of
discrimination?”

My suit of Armor is equipped with the Gospel Shield.

I am not bitter against those who still can not see that “I am of the Human race that is not going to be extinct”.
I am not bitter against those who still do not feel that I am a part of God’s Will.

“Wherefore? Because they sought it not by faith,
but as it were by the works of the law.
For they stumbled at that stumbling stone.
As it is written,
Behold, I lay in Zion a stumbling stone and rock of offence: and
whoso ever believeth on Him shall not be ashamed.”
Romans 9:32

Patricia A. Jamison
poet

“Black History”

[Elder Woman to a Young Woman]

You asked me, "Honey, ain’t you afraid in these troubled times?”

And I answered, “Child I ain’t afraid of nothing. These old bones have experienced it all. In my lifetime I have had to make gravy five different ways and had little to do it with. I have eaten possum, baked sweet potatoes in ashes and ate cornbread for breakfast, but I grew strong!

“I have given birth in the fields; came back to work in two days, fit as a fiddle in my soul but not in my body.

“In my life I had to learn to walk on ‘doctors’ cotton’ and not make a sound, sleep with one eye opened and the other watching for hate-crimes in the night.

“Scared by a cow was the answer given when a lighter than light child appeared in a blacker than black household. That didn’t matter; the child went on the block anyway. My heart became like a tree planted by the water; unmovable.

“Then Freedom came. Fairness was unheard of. The scales always tipped in favor of the owner, not me. The pencil was the boss. Voting was not for me either. The people were going to do what they wanted even if I had...

“Opportunity was something that came to other people but I still lived on, not wealthy, but wise in the art of living, loving and surviving.

“I didn’t own much so I didn’t court jealousy nor embrace envy because my friends didn’t have much either, and I had friends. My friends asked nothing of me nor I of them but to be friends from birth until death.

"So you see, honey, I ain't afraid of nothing! I have experienced it all. I was considered ignorant but I kept my own council with God and He delivered me.

"You see, honey, I was a Slave."

Gertrude R. Anderson

"We Were There"

Look at me! I came from the oldest family in time. I was here when God said, "Let us make man" and then created me, a woman to be his help mate. He didn't create me from the man's foot so I could be walked on; He didn't create me from his head where I could rule over him; He created me from a rib in his side so I could walk beside him and be his helpmate.

You see, I was there in creation. My bloodline reaches back before the flood. I was there when the Angels sang to the Shepherds in the field and brought the news that the Christ Child had been born. I was there when Pharaoh held the Israelites in bondage as slaves, and I was there when Moses led them across the Red Sea and to freedom. I was there when God destroyed Sodom and Gomorrah because of the sins of the people and I obeyed Him when He said, "Don't look back." In today's world, I will also say "Don't look back." Let the bonds of oppression be a distant memory let it fade with time. Replace it with positive thinking and good works, work that will lift humanity to its highest potential, especially our children and families.

Don't look back, to a time of ignorance when our children believed that babies came from black bags or were hidden in a cabbage patch to be found by its mother. Tell our children the truth! In other words, tell it like it is. Don't forget, these babies are ours. Don't look back, to things that keep us apart; look for ways to bring us together as a people. Work for the good of all. Help create jobs for the jobless. Help train them for what is needed. We have plenty of educated people who are capable of teaching whatever we need. Let us renew our culture of caring for our elders. Search for the wisdom they have stored away in their sea of knowledge.

Sometimes, what they say may not make sense but listen anyway. There may be something in their conversation that will help us solve many of life's problems today.

Can you recall how our older people could cure almost any illness with a big dose of Castor Oil and with different kinds of teas and tallow? Many of these things the Doctors haven't heard of – yet. God has always empowered special people with the gift of Healing.

Again I say "Don't look back!" Don't hang on to old problems. Let them go! Only we can solve the problems about us as Black people. If we work together we can achieve all that God has for us and we will be blessed. Don't let anyone define who you are and what your abilities should be. That's your job! Believe, and you shall achieve!

Just as the sun sets in the West and the Stars continue to shine, we have and we will endure. God put us here in the beginning and made us a strong people; we are blessed. We have the D.N.A., the scientific proof that this is true. Thank God for our Black Ancestors. Because of those in our past, we are with you today, because we are who they were – Beautiful, Talented and Black.

Gertrude R. Anderson

"THE OLD SCHOOL HOUSE"

(Prose)

I saw it yesterday in passing. It brought back many happy memories. It stood leaning against an old weather-worn, insect-ridden, oak tree that refused to give up its place of residence in the fertile soil that was once the school yard.

Young oaks, kindred of the mighty oak, circled its base, waiting their turn to occupy the space of their ancient ancestor. Soon the old wooden school house will return to the dust from which it came, long ago in the form of a tree.

The wooden floor wore the signs of its past occupants, termites, and had sunk onto the trash underneath. The schoolhouse now served as a home for migrating rodents, and insects of many varieties. The door hangs by one nail.

The building had once been divided by an old pot-bellied wood-burning heater. Its purpose was to keep the students warm in the winter. For some, this was true. For others, it served only to cook the legs and leave life-long scares giving proof of its use.

The purpose of the building, and the activities held there were to prepare those who attended to learn about life and to look forward to seeing places they may or may not see and dream dreams that may or may not come true.

When passing and looking at the old school building, I can almost hear the laughter and see the faces of the students who studied there, who ate their lunches on top of sawed-down tree trunks, and shared what they had for lunch.

The majority of those students have gone on to be with the Lord at His appointed place. As I gazed upon the ancient building, it seemed to be holding on until all who remembered it, will have vanished unto the ages. Only then will it give up and fall – never to rise again.

But from these simple walls, many minds have been invigorated and encouraged to be the best that they could be and make positive contributions to humanity's well being.

In the annuals of time, this place will be remembered as the place where it all began in learning about different places and different walks of life. However, somewhere in an old school house such as this was the place where we spent our time and enjoyed our youth.

"Wisdom is the principle thing;
Therefore, get wisdom
and with all thy getting,
get understanding."
Proverbs 4:7

Dedicated to the memory of the old
Tunstall School at Victoria, Mississippi

Gertrude R. Anderson

"Once Upon a Memory"

Remember when we were children, when most of us lived on a farm; how we spent time making things from scraps of wood, clothe, tin cans, and bent nails?

Remember how we climbed trees for fun and dreamed of a wonderful world outside of our line of vision, and pretended that we were characters we had read about in our school books?

Remember when the same food was cooked almost everyday, and no one complained because it was cooked with love and imagination?

Remember when just a look from our parents would let us know that a message was being sent and we had better behave?

Remember when we were told to kneel beside our bed each night and pray, asking God to bless our family, one by one?

Remember when our parents didn't have much money and we were taught to work for our living?

Remember when the top-priority, among our families and our neighbors, was sharing and helping one another especially when times were rough?

Remember when the joys in the community were our joys, and Sunday School was the place we wanted to be each Sunday with our friends? I hope you also had precious memories.

"A merry heart is like medicine,
but a broken spirit drieth the bones."
Proverbs 17:22

Gertrude R. Anderson

“Speaking of Memories …”

Lessons from my Father

(Prose)

When I was a little girl, I was taught to never do my work in a haphazard way. My father believed in teaching a lesson by letting a child do a job by themselves. I remember him teaching me the Golden Rules, “Do unto others as you would have them do unto you” and, “Don’t spend every dime you have, save some for another time.” These lessons have stayed with me. He also let me learn other things on my own.

When I was about 6 years old, my father gave me a job to do - cleaning out a closet. Now at that age, children like to play, not work! I knew better than to complain or pout, because I didn’t want to do the job. Children didn’t do that in my day, at least not in the presence of the parents. I just sat quietly and later complained to the walls of my room.

As soon as my father left for work, I began my job. With tears running down my face, I started to pick up some of the boxes that had fallen from a stack in the corner and arranged them neatly to one side of the closet. I began to sweep the closet floor and move the boxes to another place. As I moved my broom back and forth I complained to myself, “This job is too much for me. He should have had someone else do this.”

Suddenly, out of the corner of my eye something in the floor dirt caught my attention. I pushed the dirt away to see what it was. It was a shiny new dime. Now in my day, a dime could buy a lot of candy! A big tall soda only cost five cents. I suddenly felt like a rich person!

Immediately, my broom picked up speed looking for another coin. I swept in every crack and corner of that closet, but I did not find another one. That was alright. I couldn't wait to get to the corner candy store.

As soon as my father came home that evening, he went to the closet to see how well I had finished the job he had given me to do. When he looked into the closet, he laughed and said, "You did a good job. It looks nice and neat. That looks good!"

Before he could say another word I held up my shiny dime so he could see it and shouted, "Look what I found!"

That was when he said, "Spend some – and keep some for another time."

I took his advice and saved a nickel. Later I was told that he had thrown that dime in the closet to see if I would sweep it clean and find it.

My Father has been gone to be with the Lord for many years, but every time when I am cleaning house and find a dime on the floor, I think of him and the lesson he taught me as a child. That was "A Precious Memory" indeed!

Gertrude R. Anderson

"Choose Your World"
(Prose)

Dedicated to college students, on their graduation day.

Choose your world in a positive way. It is up to you to choose the path that leads to it. It is your right, and your life.

Your path may not be easy, but if you heed the wisdom that is freely given in the Holy scriptures, you will have the strength and the courage, to travel it.

There may be obstacles put in your path but for true believers, God will use these obstacles as your stepping-stone to success.

Your abilities may not be what you would like them to be, but use what God has given you. Do your best and don't worry. The Bible teaches us that worry accomplishes nothing. Remember the scripture that says, "I can do all things through Christ who strengthens me." Work on your goal step by step.

Pray for a sound mind and a clean heart. These two blessings will guide you through all of life's experiences.

As you travel the path that you believe will fulfill your expectations, leave a light that others may follow. In choosing your world, you may be helping others to choose theirs.

The world may be a little better because you were important in the life of someone who chose you as an example. GOD BLESS YOU!

Gertrude R. Anderson

"BEGIN AGAIN"

You can overcome past pain and sorrow,
Enjoy today and relish tomorrow.
Don't be sad, don't feel blue,
Just be still and let God love you.

The past is History, [His story]
Now give Him the honor, praise and glory.
He will lead you in the right path.
He will teach you all about His math.
You'll have no fear, no reason to hide,
When you learn God's way to add, subtract, multiply and rightly divide.

Study His word; the light will shine,
As the dark past is left behind.
You'll soar into a bright new tomorrow,
Free of sin's stain, shame, and sorrow.

By His Grace,
"Naomi"

About the Author

Gertrude Richmond Anderson

While preparing to write the book, POEMS AND PRAISE, Gertrude Richmond Anderson invited several of her friends to use their writing skills also. Anderson's love of reading, writing, and music was encouraged by her fifth grade teacher in the classrooms of the Chicago Public Schools.

Just before World War II ended, she married Odie S. Anderson, a veteran of the Armed Forces. She and her husband lived on a farm and reared a family of eight. Later, she returned to school and earned a degree in Elementary Education from Rust College in Holly Springs, Mississippi. She began a career teaching in the Head-Start Program, and the Mississippi Public Schools.

She said that reading was her favorite hobby. "There is power in words," she said. "Words make a person **Think and Feel**." As an example of powerful words she quoted Genesis 1:1, "In the beginning, God created heaven and earth." "When I think of those words," she explained, "thoughts let me know that there is a power greater than I am."

Another example quoted was Psalms 23, "The Lord is my Shepherd, I shall not want…" Her explanation was that "When I read this, I think about that God is the source of my strength and He is my protection. He leads me and guides me in the direction that He wants me to take."

What more could be said about the author other than she is a believer in the power of words? She is very interpretative. "The poem **Invictus** and in the movie, a person named Nelson Mandela tells a young man about his 27 years in the prison on Robene Island. He said that the poem made him stand up when he wanted to lie down." That is how Anderson said that she often felt. Yet as a reader, more powerful words invoked courage in her.

"Last but not least", she said, "when I sing 'My country 'tis of thee; Sweet land of liberty, of thee I sing...' I think that God put me here in the United States of America, and this is where I will give Him the honor and the praise.

"My book, POEMS AND PRAISE, does that. The book contains poems that rhyme and some that are written in what I call free style, some in verse, and some on several subjects."

After retiring from her career as a teacher, Anderson continued spending her time writing words. She wrote articles for the community. She also developed Biblical plays for her church's drama ministry where she wrote many poems, and praised God.

www.ingramcontent.com/pod-product-compliance
Lightning Source LLC
LaVergne TN
LVHW010542100826
845148LV00013B/2569

* 9 7 8 0 9 7 5 8 5 4 9 1 4 *